Breaking all the Rules:

How to Rent Your Vacation Home

Marie R. Ferguson

ISBN-10: 1-4196-2811-9
ISBN-13: 978-1-4196-2811-5

To order additional copies, please contact us.

http://www.howtorentvacationhomes.com/

or

BookSurge, LLC
www.booksurge.com
1-866-308-6235
orders@booksurge.com

Interior book formatting and cover design by
Rend Graphics
www.rendgraphics.com

Dedication

To John, my wonderful husband who always believed
in me...

Thank you for your support and patience
- with all my love

Table of Contents

Foreword

Marie Ferguson owned an extremely beautiful condo on the beach in New Hampshire. She also bought a chalet in the same neighborhood. I had the pleasure of cleaning both properties.

Marie was apprehensive at first about renting her elaborate condo. But, when she did decide to go forward, Marie put together a very hospitable but regimented set of rules to which renters would agree to before sending their deposit on their rental. She made it very clear to her renters that whether they were renting a cottage for a beautiful summer week and it cost $1,000 per week or a pricier home for $2,500 per week, no one has the right to mistreat your property. All of her renters respected her property because of the trust Marie placed on each of her renters and because of the beautiful, clean condo she presented to them. She never had any trouble with her renters. And, it was always booked which worked well for me since I was her house keeper.

If you have any reservations about renting because you think renters won't respect your wishes, you need to read this book. It tells you everything you need to know about renting your condo, cabin, cottage or home. Marie thought of everything! Don't worry. Rent with confidence. From the many years of experience, Marie has worked out all the "kinks" of renting. Reading this book will save you time, dollars and peace of mind!

- Lois Cochrane, Ossipee, New Hampshire

Preface

Vacation Homes: Our Special Place
A place to create memories

What better place to be to create memories with our loved ones than at our very own vacation home. We all dream about owning a second home to escape our every day lives, a place to look forward to visiting and sharing with our family and friends. It could be on a beach or deep in the woods. Warmer climates are most desirable for sun lovers. Yet skiers and snowboarders love the colder climates. There are so many choices available.

More and more people are looking for a place to enjoy, to call their own and to invest their money. With the purchase of vacation properties you are able to reap the benefits in several ways. First, you choose a location that suits your needs. If you like to play golf, buy your home near a golf course; if you love the water, a lake house or beach house would be a great choice. Second, short-term rentals have been proven to earn more income than most long-term rentals and with less damage potential.

In today's economy with the recent change in direction for the real estate market, vacation properties are becoming more affordable. With the baby boomers reaching retirement age, vacation homes are becoming more popular and in demand. Many retirees prefer to rent vacation homes for an entire season while others believe it is smart to have ownership of property and use it for rental income when they are not occupying it themselves. Short-term rentals have been proven to earn more income than most long-term rentals and usually with less damage potential.

Owning property means having expenses such as mortgage payments, real estate taxes, utility bills and maintenance fees. Wouldn't it be great if our property could pay for itself? For some of us, it is a necessity to produce as much rental income as possible in order to reduce these expenses. For others, it is by choice to have rental income. Either way, there is a way of getting the most from your investment.

Over the years, I have experienced the many aspects of renting my properties. They consist of designing the rental, screening renters, advertising property, preparing and sending out rental agreements, collecting the fees, returning security deposits and much more.

I hope you enjoy reading this book as much as I did writing it. I want you to get excited about renting your vacation home as I do. I hope you have wonderful experiences and reap the benefits as I have with my rentals. Enjoy!

Acknowledgments

To my husband, John with all my love. Thank you for your support and listening to me while I bounced ideas off you over and over again.

To my parents for always believing in me and telling me that I could achieve anything as long as I worked hard enough for it. I love you both.

To my daughter, Necole for giving me her honest opinions every time I asked her for it. I love you.

To my son, Stephen for always being there to share ideas every step of the way. I love you.

To my good friends, Rosie Rowe, Amy Blaylock, Kris Hood and Dottie Getchel who spent hours upon hours proofing my book until it was finally completed. Thanks to all of you.

And, a VERY special thanks to my friend, Anita Thomas for the endless nights and weekends helping me put this whole thing together. I couldn't have done it without you!

To my friend and employer, Buzz Burrage who introduced me to the vacation rental industry and who permitted me to spend some of my working hours on my book because he believed in me and wanted to see me achieve my goals. Thank you for being so supportive all through the years.

I also want to thank villa4vacation.com, vrbo.com, cyberrentals.com and perfectplaces.com for being the first websites to list my e-book.

Chapter One
Becoming a Landlord: Is it Right for You?

Do you own a vacation home? Would you like to earn extra income to help cover your expenses, go on a trip or purchase a new car? Have you ever thought about using your vacation home as a rental property when you and your family are not there to enjoy it? If so, what is stopping you? Are you afraid that renters will damage your property or that it will not be available when you want to use it?

That is exactly how I felt before I decided to give it a chance. Once I made that decision, I began the process of trial and error. Finally, I came up with a wonderful solution that really works! That is why I have written this book -- to share with you my proven system that is easy to follow.

I will show you how to design, maintain and rent your vacation home so you and your family can still enjoy it whenever you choose. As a bonus, you will earn extra income to spend as you wish. I believe if you follow these simple steps which are outlined in this book then you, too, can be very successful. Like so many other homeowners, you will be looking forward to those checks coming in!

After reading this book, you will be able to decide whether this is something you could do and still feel comfortable. You will be able to look at this as an opportunity to earn extra income, to meet new people and to get excited about renting. It has given me that and much more!

You have probably heard that rental property is a great source of income. But, what you may not know is that in many cases  <u>the earning potential for vacation property, which is considered short-term rental, can be greater than long-term "residential" properties.</u> You can charge a higher rate for a one week rental than you would charge for a whole month! That is because a vacationer is willing to pay more for that one week because they know it is only one week. But, that same person may not be able to afford -- nor would they want to pay that same amount -- on a monthly basis. For example: A rental fee may be $1,200 per month with an annual lease. However, a weekly rental for that same property could be $1,000 for a total of $4,000 per month! You will be targeting a whole different market when you advertise as a vacation rental. You are looking for the vacationer, not an annual tenant.

 <u>It is important to understand that careful planning, timing and being consistent is what will help you become a successful landlord.</u> It can be fun, exciting and very profitable!

If you have had any experience with long-term rental properties, you may be discouraged from renting your vacation home. However, when you compare a long-term rental property with a short-term rental, there are very few similarities! Unlike long-term rentals, your renters will be in and out of your home in short intervals. No need to worry about evictions! You will be able to check your property between each rental period to see if your home was left clean and without any damage. If the renter did not leave your home in the same condition as when they arrived, you will be able to deduct (from the renter's security/cleaning deposit) a cleaning fee and the cost for repairs for any damage they had caused during their stay. However, if the unit is left clean, the house keeper should still clean everything, making sure nothing has been missed. This would be at the <u>owner's expense</u>, not the renter's expense. The security deposit should never be looked at as another means of income. It is strictly for damages or for leaving the unit unusually dirty.

<u>Here are a few simple steps to help reduce some of the potential risks in renting.</u>

Secret
#3

- Carefully screen your renters.
- Have a clearly written, signed Rental Agreement on file.
- Require a substantial Security/Cleaning Deposit.
- Design and decorate your rental property properly.
- Hire a good, dependable and honest house keeper – or service.
- Advertise where you will get the most exposure.
- Buy a good homeowners insurance policy.

Through the rental process, I have met many new people. They have shared their vacation memories with me. It has given me the opportunity to travel to new places and to be able to swap my home for someone else's vacation home in different locations. No matter what you decide today, you can always change your mind tomorrow. The option of renting your vacation home will always be there for you.

Chapter Two
Finding the Perfect Vacation Property

Whether this is your first time buying a vacation property or not, the first rule stays the same. Find a property that YOU love!

Remember, if *you* love your vacation home, then your renters will too. Having a great vacation home will make it easier for you to market and will increase your chances of having many repeat renters in future years.

If you prepare your vacation home properly, you will lower your risks and increase your profits. You should feel proud as you describe it to potential renters.

It is not necessary to buy the most expensive property in the neighborhood to get the highest rental fee. However, you do have to be willing to make your home the most desirable rental in the area.

Location is VERY important. I cannot emphasize this enough. If you prefer to rent to families, find a location where there are a lot of activities available nearby for all ages.

If you choose to buy your property in a secluded area, make sure it is still close enough to a grocery store, gas station, bank and a hospital. Having a shopping area or a movie theater within a short drive is great for those vacationers who decide, after a few days of seclusion, they need something else to do. Remember, the more attractions in your area, the more you have to offer to your renters, the more desirable your home will be and the bigger your target market! Be careful when you make this decision. It is one that may not be easily rectified.

Summary list for choosing an investment property:

- Find a property that YOU love! Chances are that if you love your property, your renters will too.

- Choose a location that offers a variety of activities for all ages. This will help widen your target market.

- Look for local tourist attractions. This will be a great tool for advertising.

- Check out other rentals in the area. How do they advertise? What are their prices? Know your competition. See what they are doing. What are they offering? What does their property look like? Where is their location in comparison to yours?

- Consider a townhouse or condominium. They can be low maintenance and with neighbors so close, they could be a good source of security when you are not on site and a good source of rentals.

- If you choose a country setting, remember: While "quiet and private" is appealing to many, try to keep it close enough to the conveniences to which we are accustomed (a grocery store, gas station, bank, hospital, etc.).

- Do you know anyone in the area? This could be an important factor if you do not live close to your vacation home. If you need someone to check on your property while you are away, it would be helpful if you knew someone who would be willing to be on call in case of an emergency. If you do not know of anyone, you may want to hire a plumber, electrician or handy man to check on your property. It is always a good idea to have a back-up plan set in place BEFORE an emergency arises.

16

- Look for an area that you would enjoy and is well known. Most people who are looking for a vacation spot would prefer to be somewhere familiar. In order to target the largest group of vacationers, you may want to stick with the more popular communities, so you can achieve your goal of renting with less effort.

- Is the property affordable without rental income? Ideally, this would be the best scenario. However, if you are not in a financial situation to afford that, then you may want to consider consulting your tax accountant or financial advisor. He or she would be able to advise you on the price range that would work for you. <u>Tip:</u> If you check the internet you will find rental/ investment calculators to use in making this decision.

- When you are looking at property to buy, ask yourself these questions. How much work does it need to get it where I want it to be? How much of this can I do myself to save on cost? What do I want this place to look like when I am done? You should be able to visualize how the end product will look. It should be both realistic and attainable within your budget. You do not want to get in over your head. It would not be worth it for you to take on something that you cannot afford financially or that requires so much repair work and becomes so overwhelming that nothing gets done and therefore becomes too difficult to rent. Have a clear understanding of what is required to get it on the rental market and how committed you are to making that happen. Again, check with your tax accountant or financial manager.

- Important to note: even though you may want to keep this property as a long term investment, you would like to be able to sell tomorrow and recoup your original investment if necessary.

- Ask your friends for their opinions. Sometimes this helps. Ultimately, you will need to make the final decision since you will be responsible for making your dream a reality. But, do listen to what others have to say. They may have some good points. Just be ready to sort them out in your own mind.

- Always speak to your tax accountant before buying or renting your property. You need to know your local, state and federal tax laws before you get started.

IMPORTANT TO KNOW: TAXES!

Chapter Three
Designing and Decorating Your Vacation Home

Now that you have made the decision to turn your vacation home into a vacation rental, the next question is "how should you design and decorate your vacation home?"

 Old Rules

Here are some of the things I heard from a lot of landlords: (Don't Listen!)

1) "Don't buy new furniture and nice things. Stick with dark colors for furniture and carpets. Renters will ruin it."

2) "Don't spend a lot of money on things. Renters might steal from you. Just leave the bare necessities for them to use."

3) "Don't leave the linens for your renters. It would be an added expense to you. They can bring their own bed sheets and bath towels."

4) "Don't provide toiletries. If you do, the renters will use what they need and take home whatever is left. That could get costly!"

5) "No one cares about your home like you do. They will break things and destroy your house."

6) "Renters do not care what the rental *looks* like, as long as it is clean."

7) "Don't put a washer and dryer in your unit. Or, put a lock on the door so they can't use it. Renters will wash everything they own before they leave. You will be stuck with a huge electric bill. It's not worth it!"

8) "Don't add air conditioning. Renters will leave it on all the time. Another reason for a high electric bill! It will cost you more to have renters in there than what you will be getting in rent! It is not worth it!"

9) "Don't hire a house keeper. Clean it yourself and save the money! The house keeper won't clean like you do and may use it for personal use when no one is around."

10) "Make sure your rent is less than your competitor!"

Sound familiar? You are probably saying to yourself, "they're right." That is exactly what I thought too. Family and friends, whom I love and respect, were giving me this advice. Of course, I thought they were right! They were the same people that told me some real horror stories about their renters. They were the experts. After all, what did I know about renting out property? I had never done it before.

Today, I have a different way of viewing it. I knew what I expected when I was on vacation. I wanted to be pampered! I wanted all the conveniences: laundry facilities, air conditioning, television, VCR, DVD player and a stereo system. Why wouldn't renters want the same thing? Wouldn't you?

Why, then, was I bothered so much by what other landlords were saying? One reason was this. They wanted me to do exactly the opposite of what I wanted to do. Their words haunted me. <u>That is when I knew I had to throw out all of the old rules!</u> I wanted white walls and light carpet and maple furniture. It would make every room look spacious, clean and inviting. What would be the worst thing that could happen? If the carpets got dirty, I would have to clean them. If they spill something on the sofa and it did not come out, then I would have it cleaned professionally and deduct it from renter's security deposit.

The decision was made and my vacation home would be designed exactly the way I wanted it in the first place. I would not allow anyone to talk me out of it! It would be my safe haven, a place for comfort and a place to have fun. I needed to feel like I was on vacation every time I came to visit. And, that is how I wanted my guests to feel. Subsequently, some renters left notes saying how inviting my home was and they totally enjoyed the entire unit. They were comfortable and had all the amenities they could want. Not only is this theory quite different from the norm, but it has proven to work!

I traveled a lot before I bought my first vacation home. I got a lot of ideas from staying in so many different hotels. At times, I would walk through open houses in different parts of the country while on vacation to get new decorating ideas. After years of traveling, I had such a collection of ideas that I was anxious to get started on my new vacation home. There were some ideas that really stood out. For instance, when I am on vacation I enjoy colors that are light, yet colorful. They are my "feel good" colors! I wanted all the rooms to complement each other. Every room had to be uniquely designed. I wanted my vacation home to be memorable to everyone who came to visit. In order to achieve that, the design had to be personalized. I could not decorate any other way. The bedrooms were designed to look like they belonged in a palace. Renters often told me they felt like royalty staying at my home. One five year-old girl described her feelings like this, "I felt like a princess sleeping in this room!" The ceiling fans in each bedroom had lighting, which looked like it was surrounded by a royal crown. Each fan was different from anything I had ever seen. The rooms were designed in a way that was light and airy, with lots of windows and beautiful scenery, surrounded with beautiful pastel flowers. (You get the picture.)

21

Broken rule #1

<u>All the colors I picked were light. I chose an off-white Berber carpet with colored speckles which looked perfect throughout the entire house. Berber is known to be durable and cleans easily</u>. The carpets had to be cleaned professionally every year, which helped keep them looking new and vibrant. <u>I bought furniture that I loved with the light colors that I wanted -- a light peachy, pink!</u> I added colorful blinds for each of my windows, which I purchased at the local hardware store.

Broken rule #2

Everyone told me that I was spending way too much for something that would soon be rented to strangers. Although, <u>some items were expensive</u>, most were not. I went bargain hunting and my expenses were reasonable. You can make something look like a million dollars without spending too much.

Check your local yard sales, discount furniture and used furniture stores. Also, check your local department stores. In addition, most furniture stores have a "sale" room where you can buy the floor models, or miscellaneous pieces. You will be able to purchase quality furniture for a fraction of the original cost. You may be surprised at what you find.

When choosing your furniture you may want to decorate with miscellaneous pieces creating an eclectic look. Again, be creative. Check out your local hardware store and see what you could use to build your own headboards or end tables, etc. I did not use dressers in any of the bedrooms. They took up too much room and most people do not use them anyway. However, it is important to provide a king or queen size bed. As for storing clothes, I added wire shelving to each of the closets to compensate for the absent dressers. They were purchased at the local hardware store.

You can build or add drawers under your bed if you need extra storage. The room appears larger without having too much furniture in it. A chair with a reading lamp is a good choice for each bedroom. Leave a book or two to read in the bedrooms on a shelf. You can build a shelf yourself to help keep the cost down. Flowers or some type of arrangement is a warm touch to have in your bedrooms. I use them throughout my home. In general, people love to look at colorful flowers and/or interesting items and knick-knacks.

A game table in the family area is another great point of interest. It will bring your guests together to enjoy each other's company. Keep checkers, chess, puzzles and cards nearby. My renters, family and friends all said they loved it. The game table is a favorite at my home. I try to add things to it, to keep it interesting for my visitors. Now, I am not saying to run out and buy a game table. I am just suggesting that it is another perfect way to entertain your renters.

Another idea is to have the pictures in each room reflect the same feeling as the room itself portrays. A painting with European scenery, showing sidewalk cafes, gondolas, mountains, lakes or rivers happily says "vacation" to me. Or, you could have your pictures reflect the area in which your vacation home is located. If it is on a beach then pictures of beach chairs, seashells or sunsets are perfect. If it is located in the mountains, then choose pictures of cabins, rivers, mountains, skiing, animals, or different seasons. Be sure it all ties in with the look you are trying to achieve in the particular room where the pictures will be hung. You will know when it is right! Do not be afraid to ask others for their opinions as well.

Tip: Wall hangings should be hung at eye level.

Try to coordinate the colors. Each room should complement the other. They should all flow nicely. Another trick is this: Let's say the picture has grapes in it. You may want to hang a small shelf on the wall in the same room and place decorative grapes on it. It helps make the picture come to life! And, the room will too. I remember one woman said to us, "When I am in your place, I feel like it's talking to me! Everything jumps out at me!" That was quite a compliment. I always keep cute little knick-knacks with friendly sayings like, "family and friends are the circle of life" throughout the house, in the bathrooms, on shelves, on end tables, on windowsills etc. People love to read them. It makes your home feel warm and cozy. And, it reveals a lot about its owner. The renters can feel your warmth.

Broken rule #3

<u>Linens and towels are always provided in my vacation home to make it easy for renters, especially if they had to travel a long distance.</u> The last thing anyone would want to do, is to worry about providing their own sheets and towels, especially if they are bringing their children with them. That would be a lot of extra packing! What if they did not have the right size sheets? They would have to purchase new ones. I feel it is unfair to expect a renter to bring them. If you provide all that I mention in this book, then all they will have to do is "pack their personal belongings and go!" How inviting is that!

Broken rule #4

<u>Toiletries are always provided in my vacation home because they are a necessity!</u> I stayed at a ski lodge when I was younger and the owner left one roll of toilet paper

for eight of us! I thought, the rental fee was high and this is all the owner could provide for us? It left such an awful impression on me. That is why it is important to take the extra step to be different than your competitors. By providing the necessities for your renters, they will remember how easy it was to come to your vacation home and will want to book with you again the following year, even if your prices are higher than anyone else in your area.

All the conveniences I expected when I was on vacation are what I provide to my renters. That is what made me stand out from all the other landlords. I did not want renters to be bothered with bringing all the extras. I wanted them to pack their clothes, come into my vacation home and have everything they needed to enjoy their stay. *That,* to me, is being on vacation! Just think of how happy your renters will be when they do not have to bring anything other than their clothes with them. Make it as easy and convenient as you can and you will get top rates and repeat visitors. They will always remember your home more than any other place they have ever stayed. And you will continuously have your home rented!

Do not clutter your home with unnecessary items. Keep it simple! <u>You can leave nice objects out for use or for display, just be sure to place them in a safe area. Be sensible. You wouldn't put your treasured vase in the middle of the room. However, you could put it on a shelf in the corner so others can enjoy it without risking having it get broken. Sensible placement of objects will help reduce any damage.</u>

Broken rule #5

I believe that most people are genuinely honest, kind and respectful. I chose not to fill my vacation rental with too much furniture or clutter because that would make it hard to tell if something was broken or missing, for example: Sometimes renters will mistakenly take home the wrong video or something else that they thought belonged to them. If that happens, just ask them. Usually they will return it right away.

From my experience, I have found that if you leave your property in good, clean order, most people will try to return it to you in the same way. <u>Renters have often said they were looking for clean, modern and comfortable accommodations. After their stay at my vacation home, I received many thank you notes saying thank you for "sharing your beautiful home" with us.</u> Many of them said it was the nicest and most comfortable place they had ever stayed! That is the highest compliment I could receive from any renter!

Broken rule #6

Broken rule #7

<u>Washer and dryer: This is a must!</u> It is important to renters, especially those with children, and it pays for itself when you incorporate the expense into your rental rates. Imagine having to bring home all of the dirty laundry after a week's vacation. Would you be interested in doing that again the following year? In contrast, imagine if all of your laundry is clean and ready to be put away when you get home from your vacation. You would have a smile on your face and be so excited that you would be willing to make your reservations for next year! This is how you will create repeat renters.

Broken rule #8

<u>Air conditioning: For extra comfort, I added air conditioning in my vacation home. I wanted the same level of comfort for my renters as I did for myself.</u> Because

26

of high utility rates, this was another justification for higher rental rates. In my "Welcome Book" that I leave in the unit for renters, I remind them to be courteous about using the utilities: not to leave air conditioning and electrical appliances on when leaving the premises, for safety and economical reasons.

Tip: Design your home for beauty, comfort and safety for both you and your renters.

Broken rule #9

Hire a good house keeper. This was the best thing I ever did!

I knew if I entered my home and smelled cooking odors left behind or saw things out of order or if the floors were dirty, then I would be upset and would never want to rent my home again. That is why I needed a house keeper. I knew if a house keeper were to put my house back in order, eliminate any odors, and clean it the way I would, then I would not have any reason to complain. I was lucky enough to hire woman in my neighborhood who was honest, caring, dedicated and a hard worker.

Broken rule #10

Pricing: If you offer all the amenities -- more than your competitors -- and you design your home with quality, comfort and convenience in mind, then you will warrant higher rental rates.

In today's society, everyone is such a rush and because of that, they are willing to pay higher prices for convenience. They are also willing to pay for quality, comfort and cleanliness!

Chapter Four
Preparing Your Vacation Home for Renters

The key to preparing for your vacation home for rentals is to provide as many essentials as possible. The initial cost may be higher than you may have anticipated, but the goal is to increase your potential income while maintaining the quality and safety of your vacation home for your own pleasure as well as for your renters.

Here is a list of what to leave in your home for renters:

- Place a fire extinguisher under your kitchen sink and one on each floor of your home. Also, place one next to a fireplace and an outside grill.

- A first aid kit should be kept under the bathroom sink in the main bathroom. You should add this to your Welcome Book so your renters will know where to find it if it is needed during their stay.

- All blinds should be left open when renters arrive. Let the sun shine in! Your place will look larger, roomier, cleaner and more inviting.

- <u>Place a Guest Book on your coffee table for your renters to share their stories. It is fun to see what your renters have to say about their vacation at your home.</u>  Secret #7

- Use air fresheners or similar product after cleaning your unit. Freshen up your furniture with the appropriate cleaners so they smell clean all the time. It will help preserve your furniture. AND, when the new renters come in, that is what they will smell, a nice, CLEAN scent. With the freshness of the unit and the view they see when they first walk in; they will be very pleased they chose your home for their vacation!

- Keep cleaning aids, dish soap, dish washer soap, trash bags, etc. under the kitchen sink. Add a note instructing your renters to use only use the appropriate soap for your dishwasher and NOT anything else.

- Keep refrigerator empty for renters to use.

- Keep kitchen cabinets empty for renters to use. If you have extra storage, you can place your personal non perishable items in a container and place them in an extra cabinet or storage place.

- Keep trivets next to stove to avoid having burns on your counters. Place a cutting board in the most obvious area for cutting vegetables. If it is placed in the right spot, this will avoid cuts on your counter tops.

- Provide broom, dust pan, vacuum cleaner and mop.

- Keep cleaning aids, dish soap, trash bags under each bathroom sink.

- Keep two rolls of toilet paper under each bathroom sink. Always try to keep a full roll of toilet paper on holder and never less than a half roll. Fold the end of the toilet paper on holder into a triangle for neatness and style. (Just as you would find in a luxury hotel!)

- <u>Hang a three chamber dispenser in your shower for easy dispensing of liquid soap/ shampoo and conditioner.</u> This can be easily mounted without any tools. Keep  them filled with nicely scented soaps.   Also, place liquid hand soap on each sink. Using soap bars can be wasteful, messy and unsanitary. They need to be replaced after each renter. <u>A hairdryer, mounted to the wall is a great convenience to have in each bathroom.</u> Everyone loves this feature and appreciates the convenience. Mention this to your renters so they will know it is not necessary to bring their own hairdryer.

- <u>Choose the same color for sheets to fit each size bed. Use the same color towels for washing purposes.</u> This will not only save you time from having to separate wash loads but it will help keep them looking clean and crisp!  Secret #9

- <u>Place a set of folded sheets that have been recently washed at the foot of each bed</u>. This will reassure your renters the sheets have been sanitized prior to their arrival.  Secret #10 You can check with your renters ahead of time to see if they would prefer to have your house keeper make the beds ahead of time. This would be an owner's expense, not the renter's.

- Keep propane gas tank at least half full if you provide a gas grill.

- Write your house number on the beach chairs and leave them in a convenient spot.

- If you are near a beach, leave beach toys (a couple of pails and shovels) next to beach chairs. If ski area, ask renters to leave skis in outside closet.

- Leave a couple of board games for everyone to enjoy. Leave one or two decks of cards. Puzzles are always fun too!

31

- Do not leave excess items in unit. <u>You should be able to scan your unit and notice if something is missing.</u> This is easy to do if everything has its own place.

- Other suggestions: Reading books, magazines, checkers, outdoor games, badminton, a football and whatever else you may think of that will help make their stay more enjoyable. Label your games with your name or address on each item.

This is what I recommend for storing your personal items:

- Gather all of your clothing and other personal items including personal linens and pillows.

- Store all of those items in large plastic containers.

- Mark your containers with clear specific labels.

- Choose a closet that will accommodate all of your containers.

- Store your containers in the closet and lock it.

- Label Closet Door: "Private – Owner's Closet"

You can alternate using this closet for storing "renter's linens and towels" when you are using your vacation home for personal use.

Chapter Five
Pricing Your Vacation Rental

When I bought my first vacation home, which was a townhouse, the unit owners were charging $700 per week for rent. I thought that was low. After checking rates for similar properties in the surrounding towns, I found out it was the average rate. Whether it was a cottage, townhouse, house on the lake or near a beach, it really did not matter. The average price for one week in the area was still only $700. At that price, it was hard to justify renting out my vacation home for such a small return. It hardly seemed worth the effort.

Now that I knew the average rental rate, what could I do to make my unit warrant a higher price tag? I thought, if I could make my home really special and different from other properties in the area, then I could ask a whole lot more than everyone else! It would have to be designed in a way that would leave a lasting impression.

It was important to me to have my family, friends and renters feel like royalty while visiting my townhouse. I wanted them to have that vacation feeling! And, when they left I hoped they would be excited about where they had just been! I wanted them to tell to their friends about the incredible place where they had stayed! That is how I would get my repeats and new renters. Word of mouth is the best advertisement. From the letters that I have received from the renters, I accomplished my goal! Within two years I was able to increase my rental fees up to $1,800 per week. Starting at $700 per week, which resulted in an $1,100 increase per week! $4,400 per month! And, you can do the same thing.

The important thing to remember is that it is YOUR vacation home, and you can charge whatever you feel it is worth to you! Remember, it is your hard work and creativity that has gone into your home and that, too, has a price. If you put your heart and soul into making your home warm and comfortable, a place that you can enjoy, then your guests will feel the same way.

Secret #13

I believe a higher rate is more appealing because there is a hidden message that your vacation home must be better than the rest. Now, once that is established, you have to be sure that you do indeed create the best vacation home in town!

Do your homework:

- **Check the rental rates in your area.**
- **What type of property are they offering?**
- **How much do they charge for the week?**
- **How much do they charge for the weekend?**
- **How often are they booked?**
- **When is their busiest season?**

Remember: You do not have to charge the same rental fee as your competitors. You just want to get a feel for what the rental market is doing. If you have more to offer to your renters, you will warrant higher rental fees. If you follow the steps in this book, you should be able to set higher rates. If a renter sees your home listed higher than anyone else in the area, I believe most renters will want to rent your home because they will know that you are offering more than the other rentals. You can charge whatever you think is best for your property. Experiment with your prices. Advertising on the internet allows you to change your prices as often as you would like. Supply and demand is still the key. But, if you present your property as being the best choice (and, it will be, if you follow the steps in this book), then you will get better results.

Chapter Six
Marketing Your Property

Although some people still use local newspapers to advertise their properties, and some still post their properties on bulletin boards, there is no substitution for the internet. After all, the web is worldwide! I cannot think of another resource that would have the ability to reach as many people as you would on the internet!

Using the internet is, by far, the best way to advertise. More and more people are turning to the internet to satisfy their vacation needs. They make all their vacation plans via internet, right from their own home!

By listing your property on a rental website, your property will be seen by thousands of people from all over the world. It is a convenience for you and for the vacationers. And, most rental websites are user friendly. On my website, http://www.howtorentvacationhomes.com, you will find links to the vacation rental websites that I prefer which offer valuable services for owners that simplify the rental process. Take a look at a few of them to become familiar with different rental websites. Check out some of the rental listings to get an idea of how other owners advertise. You will find this helpful when you are setting up your own advertisement on a rental website.

Many homeowners make the mistake of listing their property on just one website. I have been asked by several homeowners why they are not receiving as many inquiries as I have received. The answer is simple. Your vacation home will have maximum exposure by listing your property on several different rental websites. If you receive one rental from each website, the income will more than pay for the advertising costs for the entire year.

If you have listed your rental property where a large number of your competitors are listed, you may want to look for additional rental websites with less competition. This is why it is so important to make your property stand out from the others with an eye catching title, better pictures and more amenities to offer.

Websites have become extremely popular and sophisticated over the last few years. The web will continue to be the number one advertising medium for rental properties for years to come.

Advertising on a website has many advantages:

- Maximum exposure to more potential renters.
- You can send rental agreements over the internet for a quicker response.
- You can screen renters over the internet. Ask questions to rule out potential rental problems.
- Out of state renters are less likely to have extra guests staying at your place.

Now that you are ready to rent, your furniture is in place, your pictures are hung, soap dispensers are filled and your flowers are blooming, it is time to market your property!

- First you need to get your camera ready. (Preferably a digital camera for easy viewing as well as easy uploading purposes.) Take your camera and walk around your vacation home, look at it from different angles. <u>What you are trying to achieve is to capture a picture of the most enticing views. The first picture someone sees as</u>  they scan the pictures on the rental website will determine if they are interested in your property. Try to get the view from the inside of your vacation home looking out, a picture of the family room area, and a picture of the outside of your home or area. By looking at the pictures, you want your renters to be able to get a feel for it, what it would be like to stay there and what the accommodations are like. Make every effort to show your vacation home in the very best light possible. You want to catch the eyes of your potential renters. They should look no further than your advertisement!

- Go to my website, www.howtorentvacationhomes.com and click on the vacation rental links. Check out the different property listings. Notice the difference between the sites you are drawn to and the ones you dislike. This will help you decide how you want to display your property.

- <u>Choose at least three websites to list your property.</u> This will give you the most exposure to your targeted market. Renters like to see your site on different websites. This will help assure them your property is real and not a scam. And, you will catch additional viewers.

<u>Tip:</u> Check the preferred listing on my web site. Some rental websites offer special owner advantages such as offering credit card acceptance, multiple listings on several sites, notification services via text messaging or email, air and auto discounts – all in one place.

- <u>The title is what will catch someone's eye</u>. Be creative. Use something different such as "Romantic Getaway," "Dreamy Abode," "Passionate Cabin," Charming Cottage," "Warm, Cozy Chalet," "Loving Family Home," etc.

- <u>Find a unique way to describe your vacation home and use it when you list your property on the rental website.</u> The more descriptive you are about your vacation home and the more feeling you put into describing it, the greater the chance of renting it. List all the amenities you are offering and all the extras that you will provide for them. Let them know that all they need to do is pack their belongings and go!

- List all the local attractions. Research your area and be sure to highlight anything that would be of great interest to visitors. They will want to know if there are restaurants, theaters, grocery stores, etc. close to your vacation home. The nearest airport and distances to cities and attractions are also important to list.

- If the website on which you choose to advertise your property has a lot of competition in for your area, you will have to work harder to make your property stand out more than the others. <u>Be careful not to show the same views as your competitors on the first page of your site</u>. While scenery is great, the renter wants to see what is inside the property. And, if by chance, your neighbors are listed on the same website, be sure to use different descriptions and pictures. You want to stand out from all the others! Choose a different photo, something creative. Show the inside of your house capturing the living area where everyone will gather for socializing.

40

- When you have finished setting up your website, look at your entire site. How does it compare with your competitors? If you are not happy with your pictures, then take new pictures and change them as soon as possible. If you do not like the way your description reads, then change it. Have your friends and family review your site and ask for their opinions.

Now that your vacation home has been listed on the internet, here are some important rules to follow regarding emails:

- <u>Always answer your emails as soon as possible or potential renters will go elsewhere</u>. Most of the time, a renter will go to the website, find an area they  would like to visit and will email several different rentals at once. So, the quicker you respond to your emails, the better chance you have in booking a rental.

- <u>It is important to communicate with the renter while they are in the "mood" for making vacation plans</u>. More inquiries are received on weekends than any other day of the week. I believe it is because most people are home from work on the weekends, maybe visiting friends or relatives, and talking about taking a trip somewhere. Soon after, the "designated" planner gets on the internet and starts making plans. Chances of reserving a rental are better if they get a response from someone quickly. It eliminates the frustration a renter may have if they have to wait for an answer, and/or from losing interest in making the arrangements.

- When you answer emails from prospects who are

41

interested in renting your vacation home be sure to answer all of their specific questions. If they are just asking if dates are available you can write back to them and say the following:

Sample response to email inquiry

Dear Renter's Name:

Thank you for your interest in renting my chalet.

Your requested dates are available. If you would like to make a reservation please send me your address and telephone number and I will send you a rental agreement.

I believe you will find my chalet to be clean and tastefully decorated for comfort and safety. With all of the amenities that are provided you will be able to enjoy your vacation like a king!

I am looking forward to speaking with you.

Sincerely,
Your Name
(Telephone number)

- If you do not have their requested dates available, then offer different dates. They may be able to change their vacation time. Give them an agreed period time limit, no more than a week and give them a right of first refusal. Do not be afraid of telling a second party that you have to check with the first party to see if they want those dates. But, do it quickly so you don't lose the second potential renters. Everyone will respect you more if you show you care about them.

- If smoking and pets are not accepted, <u>make sure that is clearly stated</u>. Most renters will inquire about that when they first email you. If someone asks if they can bring their pet, give them telephone numbers of local kennels.

- Describe your home as the most desirable place to be. Highlight the important features that will identify your place as being different and better than any other rental in the area. Use the words "luxurious," "spacious," "views," etc. Use very descriptive adjectives that will best describe your property. Be creative and choose your description wisely. Your goal is to attract potential renters to your property over any other property.

- Explain to the renter how much you love being there, how beautiful it is and especially how clean it is. Cleanliness is definitely on the high priority list for most renters. Mention the many activities a family can do while renting your home.

- Describe the unit's layout. Let them know how many bedrooms and bathrooms. Explain to them which rooms are located on each floor.

- The idea is to keep them interested and to find out as much as possible about them. Then, follow up with a telephone call as soon as possible for an additional screening and to make the reservations. (See Chapter Seven)

Chapter Seven
Screening Potential Renters

How to screen potential renters via telephone:

(You may have traded emails before speaking via telephone. If so, then adjust the following to reflect what you stated in your emails.)

- Introduce yourself. Ask for their name, address, telephone number and email address. What dates are they interested in renting. Ask if these dates are flexible. How many people in their party? You will need all of this information for the rental agreement. The email address is a convenient and cost effective way to send your agreements to them.

- Be friendly and warm. Get excited when you are describing your vacation home to them! Let them know how much you love it and all the fun you have when you are there. Tell stories about how much fun your children and friends have when they are visiting with you. Give them a list of all the fun things to do in your area. Be pleasant and genuine. You need to establish a personal connection with your renter. By doing this, you will make them excited about staying there and you will become a "real" person to them. Also, they will feel responsible for respecting your property thereby lessening the potential for damage.

- Ask your potential renter how many people (adults/ children) will be in their party. How old are the children? Will there be any additional over night guests visiting during their stay? If so, and if you allow day visitors, then make a notation on the rental agreement showing who and how many will be staying overnight. List everything that you both agree to in your rental agreement. Each of you should sign that agreement. This will help avoid having extra guests (not paying and using your utilities or having parties that could get out of control). The main objective is to help minimize any damage to your property. Having a certain amount of control over how many people will be there is one way of limiting damage and wear and tear on your property. You want to avoid any "surprises."

- What are their plans for their vacation? What kinds of activities are they interested in doing? This information will be helpful later when you are trying to "personalize" the welcome package. Add local pamphlets, restaurants menus, shows, etc. that might be of interest to your renters. If the renters will be skiing, let them know where to put their skis at the end of the day. If they will be swimming, they will need to know where to put wet towels, beach chairs, etc. You can list all of these things in your Welcome Book.

- Be Selective: Limiting the number of people in each party is really important. If it is a condominium that you are planning on renting, you will need to check with the association to see if they have any rules on how many occupants you can accommodate at one time. No matter what type of property, you should always set limits to how many people you want using it. The goal is to minimize the potential risk of damages.

- Decide whether you will allow pets. If you do, then make a list of rules that will apply to their pet. Ask for a "pet" security deposit in case of any damages. If you do not allow pets in your vacation home, then suggest a few kennels in your area. The renters may find comfort knowing they can check up on their pet during their stay at your vacation home.

- Talk about all the amenities you have to offer. Let them know that the linens and towels are included. That is a big plus for most renters. The last thing that most people want to do is to bring their own linens and then have to take them home again to clean. You want to make it as easy and as comfortable as possible for your renter.

- Ask your renters if they are familiar with the area. If so, find out if they ever rented in the area before. If they did, what did they like or not like about the last place they rented. This will help you understand what they are looking for in a rental and what their expectations are for their vacation. I would ask for a reference from a previous landlord.

- The more fun your renters have during their rental period, the more likely they will become repeat renters. It is nice to have the same people year after year.

- Remember, you are sitting in the driver's seat. You can choose who and how many people you want on your property. Don't be afraid to ask as many questions as possible. Find out as much as you can about your renters. The more information you have, the easier the decision will be to see if this is a right fit for you.

Chapter Eight
Scheduling

- <u>Before you take any reservations, make some telephone calls to your family and friends who may wish to stay at your vacation home. Ask them to get back to</u>  you as soon as possible in order for you to reserve those dates for them. <u>When you get the dates they would like reserved, add them to your calendar.</u> Now that you have all the reserved dates for your family and friends, you can now start adding rental reservations.

- <u>Get a new calendar that shows each month with the days of the week in boxes large enough to record your rentals.</u>

- Make sure you give your house keeper an updated calendar whenever you make changes. It is very easy to forget to let your house keeper know that a change has been made unless you have a system in place. This could create an embarrassing situation for your house keeper and your renters.

- Be sure to write the date and time of arrival and date and time of departure for each reservation. Add their name, phone number, amount of deposit and balance due. If you have room, add their email address for easy access.

- If you have made any special arrangements for your guests, (example: if you promised to provide a crib during their stay or made special provisions for them to bring a boat, etc.) be sure to add it to this calendar along with name of the renter and telephone number for easy reference. The additional information will be helpful when you are reviewing the schedule and/or for your house keeper to have handy. You will need to copy all revisions and give to your house keeper in order to keep her informed and up to date.

- Any reservations or pet or damage deposits you receive should be recorded on this calendar. Just be sure to keep a good accounting system in place. Important note: Opening a separate account for your rental property is an easy way to keep your accounting in good order.

Chapter Nine
Security/Cleaning Deposit

- <u>Always ask for a security/cleaning deposit.</u> Determining the amount of security deposit: For short-term rentals $300 - $500 deposit is reasonable. It  should be made clear that if the charges exceed this amount, renter shall accept responsibility. If you accept credit cards you may want to use it for this deposit.

- What are your competitors charging? Ask other vacation homeowners in your area. See what your competition is charging for a security deposit. You may feel you need to adjust the amount depending on your rental fee.

- Returning a security deposit: If there is no damage and the unit is left in the same condition as you gave it to them, then it is your obligation to return their deposit. You may want to check with your state laws to see if there is a limited time period in which a security deposit must be returned. It is usually within twenty-one days from the day of departure.

- When to keep a security deposit: If the unit is not clean or has been damaged in any way, you can deduct the amount it will cost you to replace, repair or fix the damage from the security deposit. However, you must send an itemized list of charges with copies of receipts. The balance of the deposit must be refunded. Again, check your state laws.

- <u>You can ask your renter if they are interested in reserving your unit for the following year.</u> If they decide to make

another reservation, (you could offer the same rate if they book now for next year) suggest that you use their security deposit towards the following year's reservation deposit. If not, then, the deposit must be returned.

- Pet deposit: If you allow pets, you will want to ask for a pet deposit of at least $100. I would make sure the deposit would take care of carpet cleaning if case any damage is caused by their pet.

Chapter Ten
Sample Agreements and Rental Packages

Samples of agreements and rental packages: Agreements should state how many adults/children are staying overnight, and the number of days. Have your renter sign an agreement and return it with a 50% deposit. The rental balance plus a cleaning/security deposit should be due one month prior to the rental period so you have time to cash their check. If rental period is within a month, then full payment should be received in order to confirm reservations.

If renters need to cancel their reservations, you will need to have ample time to get a replacement rental. If no replacement is found, you should have a no refund policy in affect that reflects the rules for cancellations. When accepting reservations, be sure to inform the potential renter their reservation is not confirmed until you receive the signed agreement and their 50% deposit.

Rental package: include only what is applicable:

Secret #25

- Rental Agreement
- Renter's Rules Agreement (if you belong to an Association, you would include their rules.)
- Confirmation Notice of Reservation Deposit
- Parking Lot Diagram, if necessary. Clearly mark your parking space on diagram. Also, your renter may want to know where guests should park. This should be clear as well.
- Directions to your property. Send clear, specific, and easy to read directions. You can map it on the internet and email it to your renters.

SAMPLE RENTAL AGREEMENT
Page 1 of 2

Rental: 7 nights 7 days
Address: 1801 Holiday Drive, Any town, Any state
Rental Fee: price
Security/Cleaning Deposit: $500.00 Security Deposit will be returned within twenty-one days providing the unit is left clean and without damage.
Arrival: January 1, 0000 after 4:00pm
Departure: January 7, 0000 by 11:00am
Number in Party: #_2_ Adults:_0_ Children
Parking Space #222 (located on second level in garage) (A Parking sticker will be provided)
PLEASE NOTE: NO SMOKING AND NO PETS ALLOWED

Name of Renter: _____Address:_____
Tel.No: (111)222-3333 Fax (444)555-6666   Email address:
Work (333)222-4444   Cell (555)666-7777

Security Deposit. The renter shall make a security deposit of $500.00 to owner in order to ensure that renter complies with all terms and conditions of this Rental Agreement as stated above. If renter fully complies, owner will return the security deposit within twenty-one days after the date renter delivers possession of the property to owner. If renter does not fully comply with the terms of the Agreement, owner may use the security to pay amounts owed by renter, including damages, cleaning services and condo fines. If these expenses exceed the security deposit, renter accepts responsibility to pay for any additional charges for all damages and/or cleaning services incurred.

- If the renter cancels, a full refund will be honored if there is an acceptable replacement for your reserved time and space. Otherwise, you are responsible for the entire amount for which you have committed. Please understand that several parties may have been turned down, especially during peak periods.

Please sign and return the Rental Agreement (pages 1 and 2) along with a 50% reservation deposit check issued to Owner's Name for (amount) and mail to the following address: Owner Name and Address

The balance of (amount) plus a $500.00 security deposit will be due on or before December 1, 2000.   Accommodations are confirmed when owner receives the reservation deposit and signed agreement. Thank you for choosing our condominium for your vacation.

Renter's Signature _____ Date: _____

Sample Rental Agreement
(Optional)   Different Associations may require the following information.

Page 2 of 2

Renter's Personal Information:
Name: _____
Date of Birth: _____

Name: _____
Date of Birth: _____

Address: _____
Do you own or rent? _____

Auto Information:

Make: _____ Model: _____ Year: _____ Color: _____
Driver's License Number: _____

Employment:

Employer: _____ Date of Hire: _____
Position: _____ Salary: _____
Supervisor's Name: _____ Supervisor's Phone: _____
Employer: _____ Date of Hire: _____
Position: _____ Salary: _____
Supervisor's Name: _____ Supervisor's Phone: _____

Renter's Signature: _____ Date_____

SAMPLE RENTAL RULES AND REGULATIONS

- Renters shall refrain from using loud and abusive language and noise levels at all hours of the day. Outdoor activities shall cease after 11pm
- No barbecues shall be used on the deck.
- All trash must be brought to the dumpster.
- Main water valve must be turned off prior to leaving the unit.
- No pets allowed on the premises by renters.
- The beach area shall be used exclusively for swimming and associated activities.
- Open fires are not permitted on the beach.
- Trash shall not be left on the beach at any time.
- Parents shall attend the beach with children to supervise their activities.
- Parking is only permitted in designated parking areas.
- No camping is allowed on the beach.

Renter acknowledges he/she has read the rules and regulations and agrees to abide by them.

Renter's Signature_____**Date**_____
Print_____

Sample Confirmation of Reservation Deposit

Date:

Renter's Name
Address:

Dear _____,

Thank you for your 50% reservation deposit for $950.

This confirms your rental from 4pm on Sunday, October 5, 0000 through 11am on Sunday, October 12, 0000. Our unit number is 111 and the key will be left in the light globe on the left of the front door. Our telephone number at the unit is #111-111-2222.

The balance of $950 will be due on or before September 1, 0000.

Please let me know if you have any questions.

Sincerely yours,

Your Full Name

Tip: Remember to call your renter one week before their arrival date. Confirm the rental dates and times. Ask if they have any questions. Tell them where the key will be (if you haven't already sent it to them). Ask them if they have any questions about the directions to your unit.

<u>Sample Refund Letter</u>

Date:

Renter's Name
Address:

Dear _____,

Thank you for your recent rental. I hope you and your family (or friends) had a wonderful vacation. Enclosed please find your security/cleaning deposit refund check in the amount of ($).

I hope you consider our vacation home the next time you are planning your vacation.

Sincerely yours,

Your Full Name

Sample No Refund of Security/Cleaning Deposit

Date:

Renter's Name
Address:

Dear _____,

Enclosed please find copies of repair receipts for damages that occurred during your stay at our unit. The deducted fees were as follows:

Security/Cleaning Deposit on Account:	$300.00
Cleaning fees:	($100.00)
Carpet Cleaning:	($200.00)
Balance	-0-

If you have any questions, please feel free to contact me at #111-222-3333.

Sincerely yours,

Your Full Name

***Copies of receipts enclosed.**

Chapter Eleven
Welcome Book for Renters

A <u>Welcome Book</u> located on the kitchen counter is handy for your renters. It should contain helpful information in order to make their stay more enjoyable. Find an attractive binder and add the following information in it.

Here is an example of what it should contain:

- Welcome Page.

- Owner's telephone numbers.

- Emergency telephone numbers and addresses and where to find a first aid kit in your home.

- Restaurant telephone numbers, addresses and menus.

- Local attractions.

- Helpful instructions for items in your home.

- Renter's Rules Agreement.

- Parking Lot Diagram.

- Pet Rules: All the do's and don'ts! What you expect from them.

- Day of Arrival: How to turn on the utilities. Let them know where the main electrical panel is located.

- Day of Departure: How to turn off utilities. Close windows and blinds, lock all outside doors and where to leave key.

Find out ahead of time (which is something you can do when you are screening them) what they are interested in doing. If you know they like to ski, you may want to leave out pamphlets about the local ski areas. If theater is their choice, leave a theater schedule for the week they will be there. This shows that you care about them. It saves them time from having to call to get information. The more fun they have, the greater the chance of having them as repeat renters. That will help keep down your advertising cost.

Please make changes where needed. Using TABS for each topic makes it easier to find! Use a nice colorful cover for your Welcome Book. Keep it on your kitchen counter for the renters to see when they first enter your unit. Tip: Find out the ages of their children and place the appropriate pamphlets next to the welcome book.

Sample Welcome Book:
Page One
Welcome to our Vacation Home

We take special pride in keeping our home immaculate and as *comfortable* as possible for our guests.

We sincerely appreciate your leaving it as clean as it was upon your arrival.

Please be courteous about using the utilities: Do not leave the air conditioner or electrical appliances on when leaving the premises, for safety, environmental and economical reasons.

All trash should be taken to dumpster (see parking map for location of dumpster).

Cleaning products are located under all sinks.

Kitchen: Please keep counters, stove, oven and sink clean.

Bathrooms: Please keep clean and dry.

Please wash all used linens and towels. If you cannot finish cleaning all towels and sheets, please leave them in the laundry room.

We hope your stay is comfortable and enjoyable. We look forward to your return! Thank You!

Sincerely,

Owner's Signature

Page Two: Emergency Numbers: Fire and Police, Poison Control Center, Hospital and, where to find first aid kit. Owner's telephone numbers: home, cell and office.

Page Three: Rules and Regulations (See Sample in Chapter Ten)

Page Four: Parking Lot Diagram (if applicable)

Page Five: Helpful Instructions

Sample Helpful Instructions:

- <u>Laundry Room:</u> Please use ONLY liquid detergent. We have a septic system and we can ONLY use liquid detergent.
- <u>Gas Grill:</u> The gas grill is there for your convenience. Please keep it clean and shut off gas when not in use.
- <u>On Day of Departure:</u> please wash all used towels and sheets. If you do not have time to finish, please leave all used linens and towels in the laundry room. Thank you!
- <u>Fireplace Instructions:</u> Use fire wood located on patio. Flue needs to be open. The handle is marked to open and close.
- <u>Wood Stove:</u> The Wood Stove should not be used, unless you have experience with this type of stove. Do not store wood inside of unit. Keep it on the back patio.
- <u>Skis:</u> Store in the shed on the front porch.

Page Six: Local Restaurants (include directions & telephone numbers)

Page Seven: Local Attraction Pamphlets (include directions & telephone numbers)

Page Eight: Marina Information (for renting boats, jet skis, etc.)

Chapter Twelve
House Keeper

How do I find a house keeper? What should I expect? How much do I pay them? If you are anything like me, you are asking the same questions. My first vacation home was located about two hours away from my primary residence so I was nervous about not always being available to clean my unit between rentals.

Cleaning companies were not available in the small town where my rental property was located. The few house keepers that I did speak with were not taking on new clients at that time. I started to panic, until I remembered a woman who lived in my complex said she was looking for a stay at home job. She had three small children and needed part-time work.

I approached my neighbor to see if she would be interested looking after my property while I was gone. She agreed to check on it for me and to clean it before and after each rental. She was extremely appreciative and I felt the same way.

<u>I gave her a list of instructions on how to clean my home, which cleaning products to use, and how to open and close my house between rentals.</u> I tried to make it clear and as easy as possible for her. I checked with local house keepers to see what they were charging and decided to pay her more than the highest paid house cleaner in our town.

Secret #27

I knew that once she started working for me, other owners in the neighborhood would want to hire her as well. I wanted to make sure that cleaning my house would be a priority. When you have a person who works really hard for you and you know you can depend on them, you really want to go above and beyond to treat them well. Without a good house keeper available, my system wouldn't work as well as it does. It is a very important part of the equation.

In order to make your house keeper's job easier, you may want to have a list of things a renter could do before departure. You could add the following list to your Welcome Book.

Secret #28

Sample list for renters:

Before departing:

- Leave thermostat on this ( ) setting.
- Strip all beds and put them in the laundry room. If you have time, please start washing the sheets. Fold clean sheets and leave them at the bottom of each bed.
- Wash and dry all towels.
- Clean all bathrooms. Leave bathroom dry at all times.
- Shut off water at the time of departure unless otherwise instructed.
- Shut off all lights before leaving unit.
- Leave house key on counter.

Chapter Thirteen
Swapping Your Vacation Home

Swapping your property with other property owners for your own personal use is a great way to be able to travel to new places without all the high hotel costs!

You can post your request to swap your rental. If you are interested in traveling to a particular area such as Rome, Paris or the Caribbean, you should focus on those websites. There are many owners who find this an ideal way of traveling.

You may want to find someone who has a unit with the same accommodations as yours so it will be of equal value.

When you find a property owner who is willing to swap with you, I would still have a rental agreement (-0- payment due) signed by all parties (pages one and two - see sample in Chapter Ten).

Be sure to request a security/cleaning deposit. The same rules would apply except you would receive no payment for the use of your unit and vice versa.

There are websites now that offer swapping. If you go to "Key Word" or search for and type in "Vacation Property Swapping," a list of websites will appear.

What a great way to vacation! One less expense to have to think about!

Chapter Fourteen
Buying Additional Investment Property

After you have tried this system and perfected your rental techniques, it may sound like a good idea to own several vacation homes! When you realize the benefits of rental income which reduces the cost of ownership, and if your capital appreciates you may want to invest in additional vacation properties.

Buying property in the same area as your first vacation home, where you already know the market would make it easier for you to manage. It would be more convenient to check on multiple properties which are located in the same area. And, your house keeper could clean both houses for you. Any overflow of renters could be redirected to your second property for bookings.

However, you may not want to limit yourself to one area. You may want to buy property in another area where you would be close to a golf course or ski area. For example: If you currently own a summer beach home, you may want to purchase property close to a ski area.

The possibilities are unlimited! Research the area in which you are interested. Review Chapter Two for purchasing vacation properties. Again, buy something YOU love!

Chapter Fifteen
Selling your Vacation Property

I had a wonderful experience when I sold my first vacation rental. The market was up and houses were selling at a premium.

I was fortunate enough to have a buyer who could see the value of my townhouse. At the time of the sale of my property, two other units were sold at market value. Yet, my unit was sold for 30% over market value.

You may ask yourself, why would anyone pay 30% more for the same type of unit in the same complex? I believe the buyers viewed it as a profitable asset instead of "just another unit."

Secret #29

The property was presented as a product. The fact that it was rented for several months in advance, all monies were collected, rental agreements were signed and received, advertisements were in place and the work was done for the new owners proves they were walking into a ready-made system.

I agreed to show the buyers my techniques. My system, as outlined in this book, was illustrated, performed and shown as an example of how well it worked. As a courtesy to the buyers, I agreed to assist them with the rentals for the first few weeks after the closing on my property.

This concept created excitement for the new owners and gave them reassurance that they could continue my system as it was set up. They were impressed by the décor of the unit, the way it was taken care of and the ability to produce income.

It turned out to be a wonderful investment for them and a profitable sale as well! You, too, can do the same thing. If you follow the steps shown in this book and create a profitable business from it, while still enjoying it as your vacation home, you, too, will have a wonderful product to sell.

All it takes is a little bit of imagination, some creativity, consistency and determination. It is well worth it over the long haul. If you decide not to sell, then you remain the owner of an enjoyable vacation home and a valuable asset. Now, what's wrong with that!

About the Author

Marie R. Ferguson has over twenty years of experience in both the financial industry and the real estate market. While maintaining her own vacation properties, she also enjoys assisting other property owners with theirs.

When she is not working or teaching others how to advertise or design their property, she can be found at her vacation home in Ossipee, New Hampshire either skiing at King Pine or cruising on Lake Ossipee.

Marie R. (Veglia) was raised in Revere, Massachusetts. Today, she resides in Salem, Massachusetts with her husband, John. They have two children; her daughter, Necole and her son, Stephen

Necole is married to Michael Tompkins and they are raising their three sons, Christopher, Zachary and Nicholas.

Visit

http://www.howtorentvacationhomes.com/

for more information, tips, and resources.

11476944R0004

Made in the USA
Lexington, KY
07 October 2011